Myanmar in Mourning: The Earthquake We Never Invited

A 30-Poem Tribute to the Resilience of a Nation
By Biha Soundarya

About the Author

Biha Soundarya, who works with a team of professional Burmese colleagues, is a poet and writer who witnessed firsthand how her friends, team, and colleagues experienced the earthquake while they were far from home. Together, they navigated the grief, the helplessness of waiting on news, the emotional weight of being unable to return, all while carrying on with their work—and still finding the strength to send aid back to Myanmar.

Seeing their resilience, Biha was moved to create this poetry collection. It is both a tribute and a fundraiser. 100% of profits from this book will be channeled directly to families in Myanmar through her friends, in hopes of rebuilding the lives, homes, and histories that were lost.

This book was born from heartbreak—but it lives through hope.

Copyright © 2025 Biha Soundarya

All Rights Reserved.

This book has been self-published with all reasonable efforts taken to make the material error-free by the author. No part of this book shall be used, reproduced in any manner whatsoever without written permission from the author, except in the case of brief quotations embodied in critical articles and reviews.

The Author of this book is solely responsible and liable for its content including but not limited to the views, representations, descriptions, statements, information, opinions and references ["Content"]. The Content of this book shall not constitute or be construed or deemed to reflect the opinion or expression of the Publisher or Editor. Neither the Publisher nor Editor endorse or approve the Content of this book or guarantee the reliability, accuracy or completeness of the Content published herein and do not make any representations or warranties of any kind, express or implied, including but not limited to the implied warranties of merchantability, fitness for a particular purpose. The Publisher and Editor shall not be liable whatsoever for any errors, omissions, whether such errors or omissions result from negligence, accident, or any other cause or claims for loss or damages of any kind, including without limitation, indirect or consequential loss or damage arising out of use, inability to use, or about the reliability, accuracy or sufficiency of the information contained in this book.

Made with ❤ on the Notion Press Platform

www.notionpress.com

Dedication

To My Friends, Team, and Colleagues—
You have been nothing short of brave and strong throughout this uninvited disaster. In a time of heartbreak and rubble, you showed courage, compassion, and resilience beyond words.
I pray for your peace and grace during this trying time. These poems are dedicated to all of you, and to the people of Myanmar, whose spirits refuse to be broken.
With all my love and respect:
Victoria Aung, Zin Min Aung, Wai Hnin, Norag (Sam), Phoo Pwint Paing, Moses Ravi, Mya Kay Zar Aung, Ye Oo Paing, Htein Lin Khant, May Zun Oo, Swe Mon Win Htut, Phyu Phyu Nway Oo, Khin Myat Noe Htut, Aye Myat Mon (Jill), Myat Thandar Aung, Phyo Wai Lin, Crystal Thanda Hlaing, Min Htet Naing (Harry), and Lewis Aung.

And to all the people of Myanmar—
This book is yours. This strength is yours. This story is forever yours.

– Biha Soundarya

CONTENTS

Table of Contents

Table of Contents (Continue)

Foreword

In March 2025, Myanmar was shaken by a devastating earthquake that shattered homes, lives, and centuries of heritage. But through the wreckage rose something more powerful—**the unshakable strength of its people**.

This moving collection of 30 poems is a tribute to the souls who endured, the hands that rebuilt, and the hearts that held on. Written by **Biha Soundarya**, a poet who witnessed her Burmese friends and colleagues navigate unimaginable grief while far from home, this book speaks of:

- The silence after the quake
- The ache of waiting for news
- The resilience of those who rebuild
- The unity of a world that rushed in to help

Read it to grieve. Read it to remember. Read it to give.

Biha Soundarya
A friend of the Burmese nation

April 2025

Preface

A 30-Poem Tribute to the Resilience of a Nation

100% of the profits from this book will go to families in Myanmar, directly through the hands of those who lived through it—friends, colleagues, and quiet heroes.

Biha Soundarya

April-2025

"Though the earth did not shake beneath our
feet, our hearts tremble with theirs.
In the face of sorrow, we do not turn away —
We show up, not just with aid, but with
humanity, with hope , with hands that hold."

- Biha Soundarya

Poem 1: The Shaking Hour

It came not with thunder,
Nor warning, nor light—
Just silence that split
Into chaos one night.

The ground beneath whispered
Then screamed through the stone,
Homes fell like petals
From a branch overgrown.

A child's toy now buried,
A mother's last song,
A prayer half-spoken,
Now echoes too long.

The hour was stolen,
The night cracked in half,
No time for goodbye,
No space left to laugh.

The earth had awakened,
But not out of grace—
It tore through the living,
Left dust in its place.

And what was Myanmar,
By dawn was undone—
The city now shadows,
The land with no sun.

Poem 2: The Morning After

The sun rose too gently,
As if it knew—
Its warmth a cruel echo
To what wasn't true.

No coffee was boiling,
No laughter, no song,
Just sirens and silence
Where families belonged.

A slipper in rubble,
A photo half-burned,
A doll with no fingers,
A page that won't turn.

The scent of the jasmine
Now mixed with the dust,
The temples are broken,
The statues won't trust.

They prayed as it crumbled,
Still gripping their beads,
Still whispering verses
Through shattered heartbeats.

And no one was ready—
Not old, not the youth.
Disasters don't knock
When they come with the truth.

The morning betrayed us,
It lit up our pain,
The quiet exposed
What the dark tried to feign.

Poem 3: Vanished

She was there just a minute ago,
Braiding her sister's hair by the door.
Now only the braid lies still in the dirt,
No feet to carry it, no laughter anymore.

He was fixing the roof, whistling low,
Now the roof is the sky and he's buried below.
A thousand names once etched in light,
Now carried on winds, lost from sight.

How can the world still breathe and turn,
When half of us have ceased to burn?
No trace, no sound, not even a scream—
Just empty plates and shattered dreams.

They vanished like birds when the trees fell down,
Like echoes that never come back around.
And all that's left are names we say
To keep them alive for one more day.

Poem 4: The Ones Who Ran

We ran with nothing—
Not shoes, not shame.
Just breath and instinct,
And fear without name.

The earth was a serpent,
It twisted its spine.
It roared beneath us
And snapped every line.

We tripped on the screaming,
We fell through the night.
No stars to guide us,
Only firelight.

Children cried mother,
But mother was stone.
And some ran with others,
Forever alone.

There's no guilt like running
When others can't move.
There's no sleep in surviving
When there's no one to prove.

Poem 5: The First Responder

I dug with bare hands
Where machines wouldn't go.
I listened for breathing
Too faint and too low.

A child's shoe appeared,
Then a foot, then a cry.
I didn't stop trembling
Until she met sky.

I've seen bones like branches,
Seen blood in the clay,
Seen fathers lose daughters
Three times in a day.

But still I keep digging,
My back turned to pain,
Because every life found
Is worth all the strain.

And even if silence
Is all that I hear,
I'll search in that silence
For someone still near.

Poem 6: The Doctor's Hands

I stitched him in candlelight,
Shaking and slow,
My gloves long discarded,
The gauze stained with woe.

His breath was uneven,
His chest cracked like stone.
I whispered old lullabies—
He was barely grown.

The hospital crumbled,
But we held a ward
Inside a school hallway,
With prayers as our guard.

No medicine plenty,
No power, no light,
Just hope and old skill sets
To carry the fight.

I lost more than I saved,
And still I go on—
Because even one heartbeat
Means someone holds on.

Poem 7: The Grieving Father

Her shoes still wait by the bamboo mat,
One red, one blue—she liked it like that.
Her cup is untouched, her laughter still lives
In echoes the ceiling no longer gives.

I dig through the rubble though I know she is gone.
A toy in my hand, but the soul has moved on.
No man should bury what he helped create,
But the earth chose hunger, and I carried fate.

The prayers do not fix it, the gods do not speak.
I've grown old in one morning, grown hollow and weak.
I scream at the sky just to hear something break—

Poem 8: The Child Beneath

I do not cry, for I've no breath to spend,
Just dirt on my lips and the dark like a friend.
A wall crushed my legs, I can't feel them now—
I count my own heartbeat, I don't ask how.

There's whispering above me, a voice near the dust.
"Hold on," they keep saying. "Just stay. You must."
I hold to a teddy that lost both its eyes,
And I dream of a schoolyard under pink skies.

If I sleep too long, I may drift away,
But Mama is waiting—I heard her say.
So I blink through the silence and knock with one stone.
I am here. I am trapped. But I am not alone.

Poem 9: From Across the Sea

We watched it unfold on a cold foreign screen,
The quake, the smoke, a collapsing scene.
We knew those roads. We'd walked them before.
Now they were tombs, not paths anymore.

Our tongues froze over in other men's lands,
Trying to reach out with invisible hands.
We wired what money we barely could send,
Wishing our prayers could somehow extend.

To watch your home crumble from oceans away—
Is to drown with dry lungs every hour of the day.
We sent tents, we sent love, we sent every small part.
But nothing felt whole. We were torn from the start.

Poem 10: The Nurse in the Temple

They brought the wounded to the monks' old hall,
Where chants still lingered on every wall.
No gurney, no charts—just mats on the floor,
And a silence that wrapped around each open sore.

I cleaned wounds with saltwater, stitched with bamboo,
Wiped tears from children who never once knew
Why the gods they'd prayed to had shattered their sky,
Or why every grown-up had learned how to cry.

A nun held my hand when my voice began shaking—
Not from the blood, but the lives we weren't saving.
Still I stayed with the ones the world nearly forgot,
Because healing, sometimes, is all that you've got.

Poem 11: The Mother Who Survived

I pulled my baby beneath my breast
As the roof gave way and we met the unrest.
I sang him a lullaby choked with debris,
But his last breath was stolen—not meant to be.

They found me still cradling what once held a name,
Wrapped in the silence, wrapped in the blame.
They told me I lived, as if that was kind—
But life with no child is a prisoned mind.

Now I sit near the shelter, they bring me warm rice,
And whisper that healing takes years to entice.
But I do not seek comfort or mercy or sun—
I only want back the small weight of my son.

Poem 12: The Orphaned Brother

She told me to run. I did. She stayed.
My sister, who danced in storms unafraid.
They said she was brave. They called it fate.
But fate is a thief when it comes this late.

I wait in the camp. They say food is near.
But I look for her shadow in every tear.
They gave me a blanket and drew me a smile—
But no one has hugged me in more than a while.

I count all the stars like she used to do.
One for the lost, and one just for you.
And when no one is watching, I still talk aloud—
Because silence is louder in the middle of a crowd.

Poem 13: The International Rescuer

I don't speak the language. I learned just one phrase—
"Are you alive?"—echoed in countless ways.
We came with our gear, our gloves, and our charts,
But it's hearts we were holding, and they shattered our hearts.

We pulled out a girl with dust in her braid,
She smiled like dawn though her village decayed.
We mapped the destruction, we followed each scream,
We worked while awake and while trapped in a dream.

They fed us warm tea with hands wrapped in grief,
And bowed in a silence more sacred than belief.
I came here to save—but left with a vow:
To remember their names. To honor them now.

Poem 14: The Lost Dog

I sniffed at the earth that once smelled like home,
Now full of smoke and ash and bone.
My boy is not here. I've looked every street.
His scent has vanished like the food I can't eat.

I howled by the river. I slept on a shoe.
Each passing human, I thought it was you.
Some pat my head, some walk right past—
The world feels too loud. The days go too fast.

But still I return where the gate used to be,
Where I watched you grow, and you played with me.
And if I must wait till the stars forget sky—
Know I am here. I did not say goodbye.

Poem 15: The Midwife With Empty Arms

I brought so many into this world,
Wrapped in towels, tiny fists curled.
But now the cries are silent and far,
As night keeps flickering without a star.

I held a newborn whose mother was lost,
A baby with warmth, but no voice, at what cost?
They asked me to name her. I named her "Grace."
And kissed the dust from her innocent face.

My hands once caught life, now they hold pain.
My eyes know too much of fire and rain.
But I will not stop—not while hearts still break—
For love is the light the earth cannot shake.

Poem 16: The Teacher with No Classroom

The blackboard cracked, the ceiling gave in,
Where letters once danced, now silence begins.
My students had dreams—astronauts, chefs,
Now all I hold are their torn paper tests.

The desks lie broken, the chalk is erased,
Not just from the board—but time and space.
I whisper their names when I close my eyes,
And beg the earth not to swallow their skies.

I still teach the wind, recite poems to the trees,
Each word is a prayer caught up in the breeze.
For as long as I live, their voices will stay,
Echoing through me, day after day.

Poem 17: The Volunteer Who Buries the Lost

I've touched more hands than I can recall,
Some cold, some curled, some small.
I never ask names—they come without tags,
Just covered in blankets, or wrapped in flags.

We mark them gently, speak them goodbye,
Even when no family stops by.
Some are buried beneath temple stones,
Some are ashes, some rest alone.

But each one is sacred, each one I bless,
With shaking hands and a secondhand vest.
For giving the lost a final place—
Is giving back just one shred of grace.

Poem 18: The Grandmother Who Remembers

This is not the first quake I've felt break bones,
Not the first time prayers fought with stones.
But this one—this one was crueler, I swear.
It stole even the sky, even the air.

In '84, the earth groaned but spared.
Now it just swallowed without care.
I've lived through loss, through war and pain,
But never a silence that felt this insane.

Yet even as I hold my cane in the dust,
I tell my granddaughter, "Still, we must trust."
For roots go deep, and so do we—
This land is broken, but so are trees…
…and trees still rise.

Poem 19: The Miracle in the Rubble

They had stopped calling names—hope was thin.
And then—
A whimper, a breath, from deep within.
A space no wider than a market stall,
Held three whole days of life after fall.

A girl with a bow tangled in her hair,
Pulled out blinking in daylight's stare.
A grandmother wrapped in a sari's grace,
Alive with dust streaked over her face.

And even a dog, tail thumping in cheer,
Found under a stove that had trapped him near.
We cried like children, we dropped to our knees,
As if time had parted with gentle ease.

The golden hour had come and gone—
But some lights, it seems, still burn strong.

Poem 20: The One Who Survived Alone

I heard nothing but my own breath and time.
I counted the cracks. I composed silent rhyme.
I thought of my mother, I thought of the sea—
I thought this must be how ends come to be.

But hours passed, and still I remained.
Legs twisted, ribs like wood, strained.
I whispered to ants and prayed to stone.
I was one voice, utterly alone.

Then—a hand, a shout, a beam of light—
They pulled me free after three long nights.
Now I walk slow, but I still walk proud,
For silence tried—but never allowed
My will to collapse.

Poem 21: The Girl Who Writes Letters to the Dead

Dear Ko Maung,
They say you were brave,
That you held Grandma's hand
Till the roof made a grave.

I put your slippers beneath my bed,
I still talk to you, though you're cold and dead.
Last night I drew us on a hill,
With no shaking earth, and time standing still.

I write these letters and fold them small,
Then place them in cracks along the wall.
If heaven has postmen, then maybe you'll see—
That I miss you, I love you, and I wish it was me.

Poem 22: The Vendor with No Market

I once sold bananas on 3rd and Main,
Now I sell nothing but memory and rain.
My stall is gone, my scale's in the dirt,
My apron torn like my shoulder shirt.

Still I wake early and sweep the path,
With no goods to offer, no coin, no math.
I boiled some tea for the volunteers near—
It's all I have, but I give it sincere.

Because when everything's broken, kindness remains,
And giving with nothing still softens the pains.
If I cannot sell fruit, I'll serve it for free,
In honor of those who came here for **me.**

Poem 23: The World Came With Open Hands

We were crumbling—body and breath—
With nothing left but names and death.
Then came boots from a different land,
With gloves and helmets, with outstretched hands.

From **Thailand**, our neighbor, came medics in white,
Japan sent lights that pierced through night.
India's rescue teams cleared broken stone,
South Korea brought warmth where we felt alone.

Singapore gave gear, **China** brought speed,
Malaysia tended to every need.
Vietnam, **Indonesia**, **Bangladesh** too—
All of them showed what humanity can do.

From **Russia**, brave teams arrived unshaken,
Their hands still steady, their hearts not shaken.
Europe reached us with funds and care,
And maps from the sky to help us repair.

We bowed with our palms at heart and head,
We fed them from kitchens where children once bled.
They came for strangers and stayed as kin,
And we found our strength from the love they bring in.

They held our babies, they wrapped our old,
They stood in monsoon, shivered in cold.
No thanks will ever feel quite enough—
But we offer it humbly, with tears and with love.

Poem 24: The Buddhist Nun of the Shelters

She walks with a bowl through the rows of the tents,
Not asking for food but giving her cents.
Her robe stained with ash, her feet bare and bruised,
Yet her chants are calm, her silence infused.

She teaches the children to breathe through the grief,
To sit with the pain, not run to relief.
With each offering given, she bows her head low—
As if prayer itself can help rivers flow.

She does not promise that suffering ends,
But that it can soften when shared among friends.
And in her stillness, the crying slows,
Like a breeze through palms where compassion grows.

Poem 25: The Survivor Reunited

I had buried my hope with my brother's old hat,
Tied tight in my pocket, I left it like that.
Then came a knock on the clinic tent wall,
"Someone outside says they knew you from Fall."

I ran with no shoes, my shirt half-torn,
And there stood my cousin I'd mourned and mourned.
Alive but broken, with dust in his hair,
We hugged like two ghosts who found breath in air.

They say reunion is a simple word—
But no sound can capture the sobs we heard.
To find the lost when you'd sworn they were gone—
Is to believe in light before the dawn.

Poem 26: What Was Once My Home

I stood at the edge of where my house was,
And the silence pressed harder than any buzz.
The doorframe still stood like a ghost of the past,
But everything else had crumbled too fast.

My wedding photo peeked from the clay,
The corner of a bed where we used to lay.
My son's height marks drawn on a wall—
All gone, like it was never there at all.

I knelt and cried where the kitchen once stood,
Where rice once steamed and laughter was good.
Now it's just ash, and twisted steel—
But still somehow, this pain feels real.

Poem 27: Streets Turned to Beds

We sleep beside strangers, on mats in the rain,
Our children curled close, too scared to complain.
The stars see us now like gods from above—
But offer no shelter, no comfort, no love.

We share boiled water, we ration the rice,
We wash wounds with salt, there's no better device.
A girl had a fever, a boy coughed all night,
And medicine came with the morning light.

Some whisper of hospitals, far and full,
But here on the ground, life is harsh and dull.
Yet still we endure, with kindness unspoken—
For even in grief, we are never broken.

Poem 28: The Fight Is Not Over

The earth may have stilled, but the war has not ceased—
Against hunger, infection, and water diseased.
We bury by daylight, we bathe in the rain,
We smile with cracked lips and bandaged pain.

Mosquitoes come now like soldiers of death,
We count not our steps—but each shallow breath.
Doctors warn gently of outbreaks ahead,
But hope is the pillow beneath every head.

This fight is not fire, nor falling of stone—
But a battle with time, and healing alone.
We may not have weapons, but we have will—
And the mountain we climb, we'll conquer still.

Poem 29: The Hands That Rebuild

With bare feet, we sweep the sacred ground,
Pick up the bricks and pass them around.
Children stack rubble like blocks in play,
Mothers mix mortar at the break of day.

We paint on walls not yet standing straight—
"Together we rise," "We will recreate."
Temples once shattered now echo with song,
A rhythm of working, of righting the wrong.

They told us to mourn, but we chose to mend.
To sow from ashes, to begin again.
And every nail driven is more than repair—
It's proof that our souls are still there.

Poem 30: We Are Not Done

Let the world know: We are not done.
Though villages fell and the rivers have run.
Though children were taken and skies turned black,
We carry this country upon our back.

We are builders, breathers, lovers, and kin,
And this is the battle we're determined to win.
Our tears may flow like monsoon rain,
But from grief comes strength, from loss, we gain.

We plant in the soil where sorrow once lay,
We forge a tomorrow from yesterday.
So write down our names, not as victims—but flame.
We are Myanmar. Still standing. Still same.

www.ingramcontent.com/pod-product-compliance
Lightning Source LLC
Chambersburg PA
CBHW040917110726
48005CB00006B/932